EMMANUEL JOSEPH

The Action Blueprint, How Public Speaking and Leadership Inspire Real-World Impact

Copyright © 2025 by Emmanuel Joseph

All rights reserved. No part of this publication may be reproduced, stored or transmitted in any form or by any means, electronic, mechanical, photocopying, recording, scanning, or otherwise without written permission from the publisher. It is illegal to copy this book, post it to a website, or distribute it by any other means without permission.

First edition

This book was professionally typeset on Reedsy. Find out more at reedsy.com

Contents

1	Chapter 1: The Power of Words	1
2	Chapter 2: The Anatomy of a Great Speech	2
3	Chapter 3: The Leader's Voice	4
4	Chapter 4: Finding Your Authentic Voice	5
5	Chapter 5: Overcoming Fear and Anxiety	6
6	Chapter 6: Engaging Your Audience	8
7	Chapter 7: The Art of Persuasion	10
8	Chapter 8: Crafting Your Message	12
9	Chapter 9: Using Visual Aids	14
10	Chapter 10: Mastering Q&A Sessions	16
11	Chapter 11: The Role of Humor	17
12	Chapter 12: Storytelling as a Leadership Tool	18
13	Chapter 13: Building Your Personal Brand	20
14	Chapter 14: The Impact of Technology	22
15	Chapter 15: Continuous Improvement	24
16	Chapter 16: Inspiring Action	26
17	Chapter 17: Your Blueprint for Success	28

1

Chapter 1: The Power of Words

Public speaking isn't merely about conveying information; it's about crafting messages that resonate, inspire, and drive action. Throughout history, the power of words has been evident in pivotal moments. Take Martin Luther King Jr.'s "I Have a Dream" speech, which stirred the hearts of millions and became a beacon for the civil rights movement. Similarly, Winston Churchill's wartime addresses infused hope and steely determination into a nation beleaguered by conflict. These great orators didn't just relay facts; they painted visions, evoked emotions, and galvanized change.

Words have the unique ability to connect on a deeply personal level, transcending barriers of culture and time. When spoken with conviction and clarity, they become more than sounds; they turn into powerful agents of transformation. Public speaking, when harnessed correctly, can mobilize communities, influence policies, and inspire revolutions.

In our modern world, the significance of eloquence and effective communication remains paramount. Leaders, whether they are activists, politicians, or CEOs, continue to shape opinions and catalyze progress through the sheer power of their words. Understanding and harnessing this power is the first step in your journey to making a real-world impact.

2

Chapter 2: The Anatomy of a Great Speech

Creating a memorable speech requires more than just good content; it's about how you structure and deliver that content. The anatomy of a great speech can be broken down into several key elements: clarity, emotional resonance, and a compelling narrative.

Clarity ensures that your message is understood. This means avoiding jargon, being concise, and structuring your speech in a logical flow. Start with a strong opening that grabs attention – a powerful quote, an intriguing question, or a compelling story. Then, present your main points clearly, supporting each with evidence or anecdotes that make them relatable and memorable.

Emotional resonance connects you with your audience on a deeper level. Use personal stories, vivid imagery, and emotive language to evoke feelings and create a shared experience. Remember, people may forget what you said, but they'll never forget how you made them feel.

Finally, a compelling narrative binds your speech together. Think of your speech as a story with a beginning, middle, and end. Introduce your main idea, develop it with supporting points, and conclude with a strong, memorable finish. This narrative structure not only makes your speech more engaging but also helps your audience retain the key messages long after the speech is

CHAPTER 2: THE ANATOMY OF A GREAT SPEECH

over.

Chapter 3: The Leader's Voice

Leadership and public speaking are inherently connected. A leader's voice is a powerful tool for influencing and guiding others. It's not just about issuing directives; it's about inspiring, motivating, and fostering a shared vision.

Consider the diverse settings where leadership is exercised – from corporate boardrooms to grassroots movements. Effective leaders understand that their voice is instrumental in rallying their teams, communicating visions, and driving collective action. When Nelson Mandela spoke against apartheid, he wasn't just sharing his thoughts; he was igniting a movement and empowering others to join the cause.

A leader's voice must be consistent and authentic. Consistency builds trust, and authenticity creates a deeper connection with your audience. When you speak from a place of genuine conviction and align your words with your actions, people are more likely to follow and support your vision. This chapter explores various case studies demonstrating how leaders across different domains have utilized their voices to inspire and effect change.

4

Chapter 4: Finding Your Authentic Voice

Authenticity is the cornerstone of effective communication. Your authentic voice is your most powerful tool; it's what makes your message unique and compelling. In this chapter, we focus on the journey to discovering and refining your true voice.

Begin by understanding your values, beliefs, and experiences. These elements shape your perspective and give your voice its unique character. Practice speaking from a place of sincerity and conviction, whether you're sharing a personal story or presenting a new idea.

To develop authenticity, it's essential to be self-aware and open to feedback. Record yourself speaking, listen critically, and seek input from trusted friends or mentors. Identify areas where you can improve and work on making your delivery more natural and engaging. Remember, authenticity not only builds trust but also makes your message more relatable and impactful.

Practical exercises in this chapter will help you identify your unique style and convey your message with confidence. Whether you're speaking to a small group or a large audience, finding and using your authentic voice is crucial for making a real connection and leaving a lasting impression.

5

Chapter 5: Overcoming Fear and Anxiety

Public speaking is a common fear, but with the right mindset and strategies, it can be transformed into an empowering experience. Understanding that fear is a natural response can help you manage it more effectively. Recognize that even the most seasoned speakers started with a touch of nervousness. Embrace your fear as a sign that you care about your message and your audience.

One effective method for overcoming stage fright is through preparation and practice. Familiarize yourself with your material until you feel comfortable and confident. Rehearse in front of a mirror, record yourself, or practice with friends to gain constructive feedback. Visualization techniques, where you imagine yourself delivering a successful speech, can also help build confidence and reduce anxiety.

Breathing exercises and mindfulness practices are valuable tools for calming nerves before speaking. Deep, controlled breaths can help reduce stress and clear your mind. Grounding techniques, such as focusing on your feet or the sound of your voice, can keep you present and centered during your presentation. These practices can transform nervous energy into dynamic performances.

Ultimately, the key to overcoming fear is to focus on your audience rather than yourself. Shift your mindset from worrying about making mistakes to concentrating on delivering value to your listeners. By prioritizing

CHAPTER 5: OVERCOMING FEAR AND ANXIETY

their needs and interests, you'll find that your anxiety diminishes, and your confidence grows. Remember, even the greatest speakers continuously work on managing their nerves.

6

Chapter 6: Engaging Your Audience

A speech is a dynamic interaction between the speaker and the audience. Engaging your audience is crucial for ensuring that your message is received and remembered. One effective technique is to start with a compelling opening that grabs attention, such as a powerful quote, an intriguing question, or a captivating story. This sets the tone for the rest of your speech and piques your audience's interest.

Throughout your speech, use storytelling to create a connection with your listeners. Personal anecdotes and vivid imagery can make your message more relatable and memorable. Stories evoke emotions and help your audience see themselves in your narrative, fostering a deeper engagement with your content. Remember to vary your tone and pace to keep your delivery dynamic and engaging.

Interactive elements, such as asking questions or encouraging participation, can also enhance audience engagement. Inviting your audience to reflect on their own experiences or share their thoughts creates a sense of involvement and investment in your message. Additionally, using visual aids effectively can reinforce your points and maintain interest. Ensure that your visuals are clear, relevant, and complement your speech.

Nonverbal communication plays a significant role in engaging your audience. Make eye contact, use expressive gestures, and maintain an open and approachable posture. Your body language can convey confidence and enthusiasm, making your audience more receptive to your message. By focusing on these techniques, you'll be able to create a meaningful and memorable connection with your listeners.

7

Chapter 7: The Art of Persuasion

Persuasion is at the heart of impactful public speaking. To influence opinions and motivate action, it's essential to understand the principles of rhetoric. Ethos, pathos, and logos are three persuasive strategies that can enhance the effectiveness of your speech. Ethos appeals to credibility, pathos to emotions, and logos to logic. Balancing these elements can create a compelling and persuasive argument.

Ethos, or credibility, is established by demonstrating your expertise, trustworthiness, and ethical standards. Share your qualifications, cite credible sources, and show your commitment to the topic. When your audience believes in your credibility, they are more likely to be persuaded by your message. Building rapport and showing empathy can also strengthen your ethos.

Pathos, or emotional appeal, connects with your audience on a personal level. Use stories, metaphors, and vivid language to evoke emotions that align with your message. Whether it's inspiring hope, invoking compassion, or stirring determination, emotional resonance makes your speech more impactful. Understand your audience's values and emotions to tailor your message effectively.

Logos, or logical appeal, relies on clear reasoning and evidence. Present well-structured arguments supported by facts, statistics, and logical deductions. Anticipate counterarguments and address them thoughtfully. A well-

CHAPTER 7: THE ART OF PERSUASION

reasoned speech not only persuades but also builds trust in your competence and integrity. Combining ethos, pathos, and logos creates a powerful trifecta of persuasion.

8

Chapter 8: Crafting Your Message

A clear and concise message is essential for effective communication. Organizing your thoughts and structuring your speech ensures that your audience can easily follow and retain your key points. Start by outlining your main ideas and arranging them logically. A strong introduction, well-developed body, and memorable conclusion form the backbone of a compelling speech.

The introduction sets the stage for your message. It should grab attention and provide a roadmap for what to expect. Use a hook, such as a surprising fact or a thought-provoking question, to draw your audience in. Clearly state your main idea and preview the key points you will cover. This helps your audience understand the purpose and structure of your speech.

The body of your speech is where you develop your main ideas. Each paragraph should focus on a single point, supported by evidence and examples. Use transitions to guide your audience smoothly from one idea to the next. This ensures coherence and helps your audience stay engaged. Varying your sentence structure and language can also add interest and maintain attention.

The conclusion is your final opportunity to reinforce your message and leave a lasting impression. Summarize your key points, restate your main idea, and end with a strong closing statement. This could be a call to action, a memorable quote, or a powerful story that encapsulates your message. A well-crafted conclusion ensures that your audience walks away with a clear

CHAPTER 8: CRAFTING YOUR MESSAGE

understanding of your message.

9

Chapter 9: Using Visual Aids

Visual aids can significantly enhance your presentation, making your message more engaging and easier to understand. When used effectively, they reinforce key points and help illustrate complex ideas. This chapter covers the dos and don'ts of using slides, props, and multimedia elements. The goal is to complement your speech and enhance your audience's comprehension without overshadowing your message.

The first step in using visual aids is to ensure they are relevant and aligned with your content. Each visual should serve a clear purpose and directly support the points you are making. Avoid cluttering your slides with too much information; instead, focus on simplicity and clarity. Use high-quality images, graphs, and charts to convey data and enhance your message visually.

Next, consider the design and layout of your visual aids. Consistent fonts, colors, and formatting create a professional and cohesive look. Use bullet points and short phrases to highlight key ideas, but avoid long paragraphs of text. Remember, your audience should be listening to you, not reading your slides. Visual aids should be easy to read from a distance, so ensure text is large and legible.

Finally, practice integrating your visual aids into your presentation seamlessly. Familiarize yourself with the technology and equipment you'll be using, and rehearse transitions between your speech and visuals. Maintain eye contact with your audience and avoid reading directly from your slides.

CHAPTER 9: USING VISUAL AIDS

By effectively using visual aids, you can create a more dynamic and impactful presentation.

10

Chapter 10: Mastering Q&A Sessions

Handling questions from the audience can be both challenging and rewarding. A well-managed Q&A session demonstrates your expertise and fosters a deeper connection with your listeners. This chapter offers tips for navigating Q&A sessions with confidence and grace. Preparation is key; anticipate potential questions and prepare thoughtful responses in advance.

Start by setting clear guidelines for the Q&A session, such as time limits and how questions will be taken. Encourage your audience to ask questions by creating an open and welcoming atmosphere. When a question is asked, listen attentively and acknowledge the questioner. This shows respect and creates a positive interaction.

Answer questions concisely and honestly. If you don't know the answer, it's okay to admit it and offer to follow up later. Avoid getting defensive or confrontational, even if faced with challenging or critical questions. Stay calm, composed, and focused on providing value. Use the opportunity to reinforce your key points and clarify any misunderstandings.

Concluding the Q&A session gracefully is important. Summarize the main themes of the questions and express gratitude for the audience's participation. This leaves a positive impression and reinforces your credibility. Mastering Q&A sessions not only enhances your presentation but also builds trust and rapport with your audience.

11

Chapter 11: The Role of Humor

Humor can be a powerful tool in public speaking, helping to relax the audience and make your message more relatable. When used appropriately, humor can break the ice, lighten the mood, and create a memorable experience. This chapter explores the use of humor in speeches, including timing, appropriateness, and delivery. The key is to incorporate humor naturally and effectively without detracting from your main points.

Start by understanding your audience and the context of your speech. What might be funny to one group could be offensive or confusing to another. Tailor your humor to suit the occasion and the preferences of your listeners. Self-deprecating humor, light-hearted anecdotes, and witty observations can be effective ways to engage your audience without crossing any boundaries.

Timing is crucial for delivering humor successfully. Pause after delivering a punchline to give your audience time to react. Pay attention to their responses and adjust your delivery accordingly. Practice your timing and delivery to ensure your jokes come across naturally and effortlessly.

Finally, balance humor with substance. While humor can enhance your speech, it should not overshadow your main message. Use it sparingly to complement your content and keep your audience engaged. By incorporating humor thoughtfully, you can create a more enjoyable and impactful presentation.

12

Chapter 12: Storytelling as a Leadership Tool

Stories have the power to inspire, teach, and connect us. As a leader, storytelling is an invaluable tool for conveying your vision, values, and goals. This chapter delves into the art of storytelling and its application in leadership. We'll explore the elements of a compelling story, how to integrate personal anecdotes, and the importance of aligning your narrative with your message and values.

A great story has a clear structure: a beginning that sets the scene, a middle that builds tension or conflict, and an end that provides resolution. Start by identifying the core message you want to convey and build your story around it. Use vivid descriptions, relatable characters, and emotional arcs to create a narrative that resonates with your audience.

Personal anecdotes can make your stories more authentic and relatable. Sharing your own experiences, challenges, and successes humanizes you as a leader and helps build trust with your audience. Be honest and vulnerable, as this creates a deeper connection and makes your message more impactful.

Align your stories with your values and vision. Ensure that the lessons and themes of your narrative reflect the principles you want to promote. Stories are a powerful way to illustrate abstract concepts and make them tangible for your audience. By mastering the art of storytelling, you can inspire and

CHAPTER 12: STORYTELLING AS A LEADERSHIP TOOL

lead with greater effectiveness.

13

Chapter 13: Building Your Personal Brand

Your public speaking style is a key component of your personal brand. Building a consistent and authentic presence that reflects your identity and values is crucial for establishing your credibility and influence. This chapter focuses on developing your personal brand through public speaking.

First, identify your core values, strengths, and passions. These elements define who you are and what you stand for. Your personal brand should be a genuine representation of yourself, so it's essential to be clear about your identity. Reflect on what makes you unique and how you want to be perceived by others.

Next, craft a consistent message and style that aligns with your brand. This includes your tone of voice, body language, and the way you present yourself. Consistency across different speaking engagements and media platforms helps reinforce your brand and build trust with your audience. Develop a signature style that sets you apart and makes you memorable.

Networking and building relationships are also key components of personal branding. Engage with your audience, both online and offline, and seek opportunities to share your message. Attend events, participate in discussions, and collaborate with others who share your values and interests. Building a strong network enhances your visibility and influence.

Finally, continually evolve your personal brand. Stay true to your core

CHAPTER 13: BUILDING YOUR PERSONAL BRAND

values but be open to growth and change. Seek feedback, reflect on your experiences, and set goals for your development. Your personal brand is a dynamic and ongoing journey. By consistently refining and aligning your public speaking with your brand, you'll establish a lasting and impactful presence.

14

Chapter 14: The Impact of Technology

Technology has revolutionized the landscape of public speaking, offering new tools and platforms for reaching audiences. This chapter examines the impact of digital media, social networks, and virtual presentations on public speaking, and how to leverage technology to enhance your communication and expand your reach.

Digital media, such as videos and podcasts, provide opportunities to share your message with a wider audience. Creating and sharing high-quality content can boost your visibility and establish you as an authority in your field. Invest in good equipment and learn basic editing skills to produce professional and engaging media content.

Social networks offer powerful platforms for building and connecting with your audience. Use social media to share your speeches, engage with followers, and join conversations relevant to your field. Consistent and strategic use of social media can enhance your personal brand and expand your influence. Be authentic and responsive to build genuine connections with your audience.

Virtual presentations have become increasingly common, allowing speakers to reach global audiences without the constraints of physical location. Mastering virtual presentation tools, such as video conferencing software and webinars, is essential for effective online communication. Practice using these tools to ensure smooth and professional virtual presentations.

CHAPTER 14: THE IMPACT OF TECHNOLOGY

Embrace emerging technologies, such as artificial intelligence and augmented reality, to enhance your public speaking experience. These technologies offer innovative ways to engage your audience and create immersive experiences. Stay informed about the latest trends and explore how they can be integrated into your presentations to stay ahead in the evolving landscape of public speaking.

15

Chapter 15: Continuous Improvement

Public speaking and leadership are lifelong pursuits that require continuous learning and self-improvement. This chapter emphasizes the importance of seeking feedback, reflecting on your experiences, and setting goals for your development. Even the best speakers never stop growing and refining their skills.

First, actively seek feedback from trusted sources. Constructive criticism from peers, mentors, and your audience can provide valuable insights into areas for improvement. Be open to feedback and use it as a tool for growth. Record your speeches and review them critically to identify strengths and weaknesses.

Reflect on your experiences and learn from them. After each speaking engagement, take time to evaluate what went well and what could be improved. Consider factors such as audience engagement, message clarity, and delivery style. Use these reflections to inform your future presentations and build on your successes.

Set specific and achievable goals for your development as a speaker and leader. Whether it's improving your vocal delivery, mastering a new technology, or expanding your audience, having clear objectives will guide your efforts and keep you motivated. Break down your goals into actionable steps and track your progress.

Lastly, invest in continuous learning. Attend workshops, read books,

CHAPTER 15: CONTINUOUS IMPROVEMENT

and seek out opportunities to learn from other speakers and leaders. Stay curious and open-minded, and never stop striving for excellence. Continuous improvement is the key to sustaining your impact and achieving long-term success in public speaking and leadership.

16

Chapter 16: Inspiring Action

Ultimately, the goal of public speaking and leadership is to inspire action. This chapter explores strategies for motivating your audience to take meaningful steps toward positive change. A clear call to action, the power of passion, and empowering others to become agents of change are essential components of inspiring action.

A clear call to action is crucial for guiding your audience toward the desired outcome. Clearly articulate what you want your audience to do, whether it's supporting a cause, adopting a new behavior, or joining a movement. Provide specific and actionable steps that are easy to follow and implement.

Passion is a powerful motivator. When you speak with genuine enthusiasm and conviction, your energy can inspire others to share your vision and take action. Passionate delivery not only engages your audience but also demonstrates your commitment to the cause. Show your audience why the issue matters and how their actions can make a difference.

Empower your audience by providing them with the knowledge, tools, and resources they need to take action. Offer practical advice, share success stories, and provide access to support networks. Empowered individuals are more likely to feel confident and motivated to contribute to the cause.

Lastly, create a sense of urgency. Highlight the importance of taking action now rather than later. Use compelling evidence and stories to illustrate the impact of immediate action. By inspiring a sense of urgency, you can mobilize your audience to act swiftly and effectively. Inspiring action is about moving people from awareness to engagement and ultimately to impactful change.

17

Chapter 17: Your Blueprint for Success

In the final chapter, we bring together the lessons and strategies from the book into a cohesive action plan. This chapter provides practical advice for applying the principles of public speaking and leadership in your own life, ensuring that you can inspire real-world impact and lead with confidence.

Start by setting clear goals for your public speaking and leadership journey. Define what success looks like for you and outline the steps needed to achieve it. Create a roadmap that includes short-term and long-term objectives, and regularly review and adjust your plan as you progress.

Develop a personal growth strategy that includes continuous learning, seeking feedback, and reflecting on your experiences. Stay committed to improving your skills and expanding your knowledge. Attend workshops, read books, and learn from other successful speakers and leaders.

Build a strong network of supporters and mentors who can provide guidance, encouragement, and opportunities for growth. Surround yourself with people who share your vision and values, and collaborate with them to amplify your impact. Networking is essential for building relationships and creating opportunities for influence.

Finally, lead with integrity and authenticity. Stay true to your values and principles, and always strive to make a positive difference in the lives of others. Your actions and words should align with your message, and your leadership

CHAPTER 17: YOUR BLUEPRINT FOR SUCCESS

should inspire trust and respect. By following this blueprint, you can achieve lasting success and inspire real-world impact through public speaking and leadership.

The Action Blueprint: How Public Speaking and Leadership Inspire Real-World Impact

In a world where words hold the power to transform lives, "The Action Blueprint" delves into the art and science of public speaking and leadership. This compelling guide explores how effective communication can drive change, mobilize communities, and inspire action.

Through vivid historical examples and practical insights, readers will uncover the secrets behind memorable speeches and influential leaders. From mastering the techniques of persuasion to crafting an authentic voice, this book offers a comprehensive toolkit for anyone looking to make a meaningful impact.

Discover how great orators like Martin Luther King Jr. and Winston Churchill harnessed the power of their words to shape nations. Learn the anatomy of a great speech, the role of humor, and the importance of storytelling in leadership. With step-by-step guidance on overcoming fear, engaging audiences, and leveraging technology, "The Action Blueprint" empowers readers to lead with confidence and authenticity.

Whether you're a seasoned speaker or just starting your journey, this book provides the strategies and inspiration needed to elevate your public speaking and leadership skills. Embrace your potential to influence and drive positive change with "The Action Blueprint."

www.ingramcontent.com/pod-product-compliance
Lightning Source LLC
LaVergne TN
LVHW020740090526
838202LV00057BA/6153